US Rowing
Youth Nationals
2015

Vincenzo Berghella

Copyright Page

Copyright year: 2015

Copyright notice: by Vincenzo Berghella

ISBN No: 978-0-578-17113-5

June 12, 2015, Friday
US Rowing Youth Nationals Championships,
  Nathan Benderson Park, Sarasota-Bradenton, Florida

He is in second place! Yes, he can do it! The first guy is about 2-3 boats ahead, hard to catch. But the first two qualify for the semifinals, so our son Andrea is doing great! Will he make it? But wait… how did we get here in Sarasota, Florida, to the 2015 Youth National Rowing Championships in the first place?

Spending time with your loved ones is one of the keys to being happy. I'm delighted to be here on this trip with our son Andrea. He is a lanky 17 years old, long legs like his mother, just 170 pounds spread thin over a 6 feet 4 inches frame. He was made for rowing.

Andrea has always been a good athlete. As I often say, there is no parent who does not ruin his children. In the good sense of the phrase, I mean. For example, I like soccer, grew up playing it everyday, and watching it regularly with my dad, in Italy. I do not think I ever pushed Andrea or his brother Pietro, two year younger, to play soccer. But they naturally gravitated first to that sport. Emulating our parents is a common, natural occurrence.

Andrea is actually a decent midfielder. He is smart. He understands the game well. He has accurate, brilliant passes in soccer matches. His high school team did well last year. Thanks also to a good goalie – Pietro, they got very close to making the playoffs. But Andrea, while a very good player, is not a soccer star.

He is actually very good at several sports. He is good at basketball. He can play well volleyball, and especially beach volley. He is a great runner. Every summer he trains hard, and in August, back at soccer school camp, he is among the fastest runners, usually the top five of the bunch of over 20.

Andrea and his brother Pietro have been to many national chess tournaments. Yes, United States National Chess tournaments. We have been to San Diego, Nashville, Minneapolis,

Atlanta, etc. In elementary and middle school, Andrea (as well as his brother) was for sure within the best 50 or so best chess players for his age in the US. I still remember the great wins, the losses against Russian-, Indian-, Chinese-American kids.

I'm at the starting line. Aaron, Andrea's star rowing coach, has let me borrow his bike. So I did the 3-4 kilometers from where we launched Andrea's boat, to this starting line. The Heat before his, Heat 1, goes. After a few minutes the loud speaker starts announcing the boats for Heat 2. It's going to start in a minute, on time, at 8:32am. I am so excited! His name is communicated on the loud speaker!

Andrea is used to excellence. He is a top student at Germantown Friends School, his high school just outside Philadelphia. He has been an excellent student since he was in elementary and middle school, at The Philadelphia School. He indeed has been a wonderful son and person since birth. Calm, collected, smart, dedicated.

I will never forget his speech for middle school graduation. He spoke about 'I'm a totipotential stem cell.' As an eighth grader!! His point was that he was an organism in evolution, capable still of becoming anything. His school was helping to discern his strengths, his best potentials. He was looking forward to life, to discovering what he would specialize in as a cell and as a man, to best help humanity.

The line up for Mens Youth 1x Heat 2 is:
- Bow 2,   W Wrobel,   River City
- Bow 3,   A Berghella,   Germantown Friends
- Bow 4,   A Morley,   Seattle RC
- Bow 5,   J Sterner,   Culver
- Bow 6,   E Sammons,   Saratoga

So Andrea is in bow (lane) 3, with probably the best rower in bow 4 – from Seattle, who we do not know. I've seen the rower in bow 5, from Indiana, before, when he launched his boat just after

Andrea's. He must be 6'6", tall and lanky, dirty blond, a good-looking boy. I fear right away these two will be the ones to beat.

This trip all started at home, in Philadelphia, on June 11th, 2015. I came back early in the afternoon from work, all excited. Andrea had his last day of school. He will, once again, bring back a report of straight A's. He has never seen anything other than A's in his school career so far. Life is not perfect, but he certainly aims for perfection. Nothing less.

This time we want to make sure he does not forget is 'butt pad,' and his contact lenses, as he did last week when he and I went to Virginia for another national rowing competition. We have already prepared our carry-on luggage the evening before. Actually, I have prepared mine; Paola has mostly prepared Andrea's.

I've been looking forward to this trip for a while. Andrea qualified for this ultimate of the national races after his Philadelphia City Championships, on May 3, 2015. He then finished an astonishing second. Only a Germantown Academy senior, Zachary Burkhart, got ahead of him. This is most impressive if one thinks that Philadelphia is in a way the US city with the most high school rowing tradition, and teams. And Zachary is a senior, in his 4th and last year of high school. Andrea is a junior still in his 3rd year.

I have left the bike that took me here to the start on the side. I walk closer to the starting line, to take better pictures of Andrea and his companions racing. They all line up perfectly. Andrea seems in complete control of his boat. He can steer it however he wants. A few moments after pronouncing their names, the loud speaker announces, "7 minutes!"

When did this rowing mania all started? How did we get here? Andrea's high school, Germantown Friends School, in short GFS, did not even have a team until this year. Andrea was always busy with school and many other sports and activities. Among other sports, Andrea is an excellent swimmer. He did regional races, even the Eastern Swimming Championships, meaning the finals for the Eastern part of the United States, where some of the strongest swimmers are.

One of his best swimming buddies is Emmett. Emmett is a year older than Andrea, and goes to a different school. Andrea has always looked up to him. Emmett is sculpted. His body could be used in an anatomy class. His muscles are all evident, starting from a flawless six-pack.

That was maybe what attracted Andrea to rowing. Emmett is also always in a good mood. His body is enviable, and Andrea prides himself in being in good shape. Emmett's muscles remained more evident than Andrea's despite they were both swimming most days of the week. Emmett must have told positive things to Andrea about rowing.

Next we know it, Andrea discovers in 10th grade that GFS, his high school, despite not having a rowing program, does have a few students who do row. He inquires, gets information. He signs himself for a Learn to Row program. With this in his belt, he is accepted in the spring of his second year of high school to Bachelor's Club.

His start today is not the best. The boy from Seattle in bow 4 gets out in front right away. Andrea, as his usual, does not have a strong start. In fact even the boy in bow 2, where in general one would not expect a fast rower, gets out in front of Andrea. I continue to video the race, getting ever more anxious. As the start is quick and the boats cannon out of starting line, I run to the bike. Of course during these few seconds my recording is terrible.

At Bachelor's, one of the premier Rowing Boat Houses on the Schuylkill River in Philadelphia, there is a program which accepts students from those schools who do not have a rowing program themselves. So there are high school kids from over 10, 20 different schools.

Jamie is the coach at Bachelor's. He is actually a good influence for Andrea. He teaches him the basics. As Andrea is the only heavyweight rower from GFS, he has to ride in a single.

Heavyweight in high school is someone who weighs more than about 160 pounds.

Here hard workouts, tough training sessions, a lot of yelling from the coach all started. Rowing with snow on the side of the river, with rain, with scorching heat, or first thing in the morning at 5:30am, or at the warmest hours of the day, or with gusting winds. Andrea got his first taste of how tough rowing is at Bachelor's, with Jamie.

He began to come back home with his hands bloody, full of blisters. Rowing is hard. Paola pleated for gloves, or some kind of protection, maybe at least taping. But that is not what rowing is all about. You have to feel the pain. You have to suffer to improve. Andrea's hands soon became unwatchable, full of blisters, callouses, swellings of blood and serum.

No pain, no gain. And it all paid off. Jamie signed up Andrea at the end of the season for the Philadelphia City Championships, a huge event on the Schuylkill River, where Andrea always has trained, and where all of Philadelphia rowing takes place. This is when I begin to ride a bike along the course, from start to finish, to cheer Andrea on all the way. I discover soon that Jamie does the same, except the cheering.

Unexpectedly, Andrea wins his first major race. He is 2014 Philadelphia Novice City Champion. His first rowing medal. Gold. We are all delighted. More than anything else, Andrea seems to truly enjoy the sport. The dedication it requires. The time on the river. The hard work.

Then I bike up to the rowers in Heat 2 quickly, riding with no hands and getting good video recording. Andrea is catching up to the lane 2 rower; lane 4 is still up front. Before the 500 meters mark, Andrea is past the lane 2 rower, in a solid second! The yellow boat of the Indiana guy I fear in lane 5 is behind, but holding steady.

Lane 4 rower gains up front, and seems in full control after 500 meters, as at 1,000. Andrea looks smooth, and while he is about two boat-lengths behind the lead, he is front of the other three rowers, confident, at 1,000 and at 1,250 meters. This race is so long! I'm sweating just biking. I'm just filming, not yelling, there is no need to.

After 1,250, and before 1,500, the race starts to change. The money in this heat is all into getting into one of the first two spots. Nothing else matters. Third or fourth, or maybe even fifth, would still get one into the 'Reps.' These are races on Saturday morning where one could still qualify from to get into the Semifinals.

But that is not ideal. The Semifinals are Saturday early afternoon, and so one would have to race twice in one day, in this humid heat, if not finishing 1st or 2nd in these initial Heats. These are brutal races, nobody wants to do two in a day, if it can be avoided.

Lane 5 begins to pull closer to Andrea. While at the 500 and 1,000 meters there is even some light between their boats – meaning about a meter or two between the stern of Andrea and the bow of lane 5, at 1,250 meters that space is gone, and soon I can tell lane 5 is gaining, fast.

I begin to yell. "Go Andrea go!" "Spacca Andrea, spacca!" "Dai Andrea!!" (in Italian). But I can see the inevitable coming. Just before the 1,500 mark, lane 5 boat has not only caught up to Andrea, but is steadily passing it. For a moment, they are leveled. I yell harder. But I also say "Bravo Andrea!!!" as he is doing well. The other guy just has an extra gear Andrea does not seem to have.

Andrea has always been a single rower. His coaches have tried to pair him up in the past, but without success. None of his classmates or teammates are as fast. It's actually a bit complicated for me to understand all the lingo of rowing, basically a different language.

A boat with just one single rower is designated '1x,' or single. One with two rowers, a '2x,' or 'double' or 'pair.' One with four rowers a '4x,' or quad or four. One with 8 rowers an '8x,' or an 'eight.' It's a whole new vocabulary. I get confused all the time. I'm lucky I guess Andrea does a single, there is less to learn.

The part of the boat going forward is called the bow. The part following the rower as he goes is the stern. Sculling means each rower has two oars, one per hand. Sweeping means each rower has just one oar, on his/her right or left, holding it with both hands. A single can only do sculling. An eight does only sweeping. A '2x' can do sculling – called a pair, or sweeping, called a double. A '4x' can do sculling – called a quad, or sweeping - called a four.

And there is a lot more secret lingo. In an eight, the ones – two - near the stern are called 'stroke,' while the ones near the bow are called bow. In the middle, they are called by the number of their seat – 3, 4, 5, 6 - , and also other names I do not even know yet. I know the ones in the middle give the power to the boat.

Lane 4 boat from Seattle sails easily to the finish lane, his win never a moment in question in the whole race. At the 1,750 meters, it is clear Andrea does not have enough to catch up to the speed of lane 5, who gets in second.

I'm so proud of Andrea. He did great. I yell "Bravo Andrea" a few times, at the top of my lungs. I see him bending over his boat, spent from the great effort.

Here are the official results for Mens Youth 1x Heat 2:
- 1. Bow 4,   A Morley,   Seattle RC,   7:40:900
- 2. Bow 5,   J Sterner,   Culver,   7:47:900
- 3. Bow 3,   A Berghella, Germantown Friends, 8:00.200
- 4. Bow 6,   E Sammons,   Saratoga,   8:06:450
- 5. Bow 2,   W Wrobel,   River City,   8:18:360

Back at the launch, as he is putting his boat down, Andrea spots the guy who came in 2nd. He walks over and congratulates this tall guy from Indiana. Andrea has won the race for me! A gesture likes this tells me his mother and father have done a good job. Actually, probably a big part of him being such a good person has been his schooling at The Philadelphia School for elementary and middle school, and at Germantown Friends High School. I am so proud to be his dad. He is a true superstar of a human being in my eyes.

Andrea has done well. Still, I would love him to do better in those last 500 meters. There is where he lost at Cooper. The Scholastic Nationals on the Cooper River in New Jersey were the other big US High School National race Andrea did this spring of 2015. There, I had witness something similar to what happened today. In fact, even more heart-wrenching.

Andrea did great, and got to the finals of his first-ever national rowing race. He was 2nd most of the race, all the way up to the 1,400 meters mark, in a 1,500 meters race. But, just in the last few meters, his long-time rivals, Anthony Williams from Friends Select, and Zachary Burkhart from Germantown Academy, inexorably passed him. He came in 4th, 4 seconds from the 1st - a guy from Miami from a club called Belen who seemed to win all the races and had the biggest crowd cheering; 0.7 seconds from the 2nd; and 0.3 seconds from the 3rd! Nonetheless, afterwards, he was not disappointed; he had a great race and did his best.

I spend the rest of the day, and the next early morning, telling him to give 100% and more in the last 500 meters of these 2,000 meters (2km) races. This is definitively a part of the race he can improve on. That's what life is all about. Play and hard work on something important; feedback and training to reach mastery; leading to eventual recognition.

Andrea has done well with his rowing races all spring long. He came 2nd at Philadelphia City Championships on May 2, 2015. He competed on May 15 and 16, 2015, at Stotesbury Cup Regatta ('Stotes' for the crew aficionados), the biggest high school race in the world, right in Philadelphia, and placed 11th overall. I remind you Andrea is just a junior, a year younger than most other rowers, who are seniors.

The US Scholastic Nationals on the Cooper River, also called the SRAA National Championship Regatta, on May 22 and 23, 2015, in New Jersey, is a huge national race, second perhaps in importance only to these US Youth Scholastic Nationals in Florida.

Andrea came in 4th, and was very close to come in 2nd. On the wave of these successes, his GFS coach Aaron even proposed to us to go to Virginia, to the US National Schools' Championship Regatta.

This regatta was the first occasion for a trip with Andrea to a race needing overnight stay. An opportunity for bonding. But only another rower signed up for the men's single. So Andrea got directly to the final, and won by about 10 boat lengths. Not a true race really, but I guess a bit of a boost to morale. The first gold medal at a national event.

As we study the heat sheets, roam around the beautiful venue of these Florida US Rowing Youth Nationals, and talk with coach Aaron, we begin to understand better how these events work. At least for the single boat events Andrea is competing in.

A total of 22 men rowers have signed up for the single races. They are initially divided on Friday morning in four Heats. Each of these Heats has a maximum of 6 rowers each. The Heats occur on Friday around 8am to 9am. The first two from each Heat qualify for the Semifinals, which are Saturday afternoon around 2:44pm and 2:52pm. Two semifinals. So eight of the twelve rowers in the two semifinals qualify directly from the Heats.

The other four are selected from the 'remedial' races, called 'Reps.' The 3rd, 4th, and 5th from each Heat qualify for these Reps. There are then two Reps, Rep 1 and Rep 2, with again 6 rowers in each. A bit complex, but it seems fair and clear, like most things in the US in general.

Coach Aaron has been helpful and friendly all day long. I'll be forever thankful he came down just for Andrea, all the way to Florida. Moreover, he drove down in his truck, with his whole family. Wife Carole, daughter Graciela about 5 years old, and one-year old son, Bodhi. When we first met them on Thursday night, as we arrived at the venue to check it out around 8:30pm, just off the plane, they were already there, exhausted.

Aaron had already done all the unloading of the truck, and prepared Andrea's boat. Priceless. Friday morning, I got to help out just a bit, and Aaron said I was now the Assistant Coach. I felt honored, but really Aaron quietly and professionally did over 99% of the hard work to prepare all the races, the equipment, and the rower, all weekend.

So our Saturday, the next day, could be really busy, with a Rep race in the early morning, scheduled again between 8am and 9am, and the possibility to make it to the Semifinals in the afternoon. Aaron suggests I keep Andrea away from the warm weather, and also off his feet. He suggests a movie.

Andrea gets a big waffle just after the race, Aaron also gets a bite with us, I eat little. We get back to the hotel, where Andrea showers. Then we come back to see John Kairys' daughter race. He is a friend of mine, an endocrine surgeon at Jefferson, the University Hospital where I work. He had texted me back in Philadelphia that he saw Andrea was racing at Nationals. He is very caring. I admire him a lot.

I'm happy Andrea gets to speak with my colleague John. Andrea has been saying already for many years, at least since 7th grade, that he wants to study medicine when he grows up. John is a wonderful man, and he tells him about diagnosing cancer, cutting away the thyroid and lymph nodes, curing people from disease. John is a perfect role model for Andrea. Calm, collected, compassionate, precise. He says surgeons like to fix things, and that is what he does and what he likes.

The rest of the day on Friday Andrea and I take it very easy. We get something to eat. We relax in the hotel. We go to the movies around 5pm. Andrea picks 'Kingsmen,' an action-packed British thriller, with some comedy, a good flick we both enjoy, save for a bit too much violence for my taste.

We pick up some groceries, mostly for breakfast the next couple of days. Once back at the hotel, we watch just the first quarter of the NBA Finals, game 4, between the Cleveland Cavaliers and the Golden State Warriors. Andrea is usually the one who never wants to go to sleep at night. But he is concentrated, dedicated. He knows we have to wake up once again at 5:45am tomorrow morning. Our lights go off at 9:30pm.

It's Saturday June 13, 2015. It's going to be a big important day. Wake up call at 5:45am. In the middle of the night for Andrea. His Rep race is at 8:07am. It's the latest we can afford. We have calculated every minute of the morning in detail the night before.

We bought breakfast already. Greek yogurt and granola cereal, so we do not even stop by the hotel-included breakfast, which had poor choices anyway as per Friday morning. By 6:15am we want to be out of the hotel room. By 6:37am we want to be at the National Rowing Center, the minimum one and a half hour before the race.

The sunrise is unbelievable. Pink and orange. I take a great picture as we are driving to the race venue. One would think that arriving at 6:35am or so would see us here among the first ones.

But this is a special morning. The eights could not race last night, as there was a thunderstorm and the last 11 races were cancelled. So there are already probably a thousand or more people here. Consider 3-4 family members per rower, plus coaches and assistant coaches, trainers, school officials, officials for the races, for these 8-men or 8-women boats, plus coax men and coax women, and you see why the parking lot is already more than half full!!

I begin to get a sense of the families who gravitate to this sport. It's clear these are mostly white. The mothers are impressive are they are all so similar. Tall, thin, long legs. Many blondes. Even the coaches are all tall, probably all former rowers.

The cheering on the water starts soon after 7am, as the first eight race starts. I watch a few of them. One must say, even if Andrea is in a single, that these eight-rower boat races are the best. They fly on the water. They are elegant. Teamwork is always better than working by oneself. The efforts multiply. The coax men, but even more the coax women, scream their directions as well as curses and obscenities at the top of their lungs. Their yells whip the heads of the rowers into giving more, more, until exhaustion.

I initially respect the rules of not going in the athletes-only area. All entrances are manned by officials, and I could not get in even if I wanted to. I do not have the yellow or light blue wristband all coaches and rowers have.

But, about 35 minutes before the race is to start, I cannot help but wander over again to the fenced area nearest the launching. There is a guard manning the gate nearby, but I do see a space between the free-standing metal fences. While the official is looking at his phone, I sneak in with the bicycle, and lock it to the Canistoga – another team from the Philadelphia area Aaron is friends with - trailer, as I did the day before.

Andrea and coach Aaron appear after five minutes at the same place near the launch where yesterday they had left the boat. This time I decide to just observe them. After all, this is a crucial moment and should be left to them, just the athlete and the coach. I may be doing it also for good luck, as I do not know if my being there distracted Andrea yesterday more than helped him.

Usually actually Andrea's coach demands them to be at the race at least two hours before. There is so much to do before the race. Rigging the boat takes quite a bit. Rigging the boat means putting it back together, with its many nuts and bolts for the rigger, the piece that holds the oars. Stretch. Run. Pep talk by the coach. Last bathroom break.

Then, Andrea and Aaron hurl the boat on their shoulders, and carry it to the dock. It gets accurately checked by the officials. Today they are even going to weigh Andrea. Yesterday and everyday they will also weigh the boat. In fact Andrea's boat was too light yesterday, and Aaron had to put some weights in it to make it comply to standards.

Then coach Aaron and Andrea gently put the boat on the water by the dock. The boat is light, seeming very unstable. With one foot in it, Andrea fastens the bolts for the oarlocks, which hold the oars in place. The butt piece goes on the seat. The oars slip in their place.

Swiftly and carefully, it's time for Andrea to get in the boat. Once he sits, one can tell he is on complete control. Suddenly, the boat appears stable. He is concentrated on the tasks. He never smiles.

The coach whispers the last recommendations in his right ear, the one closer to the dock. I wave my last 'good luck Andrea,' as his boat leaves the dock and seems to float on the calm, still water.

Once Andrea has pulled off the launch, I do walk over Aaron, the coach. He is concerned a bit, as Andrea seemed tired to him. I reassure him Andrea slept well. He is probably just concentrated. He is not one to smile and be cheery, especially before an important event.

Aaron is nice again to let me borrow his bike. I ride quickly to the starting line. Andrea is in Mens Youth 1x Rep 2. I get there in time to see the boats line up. Each of their boats has their name called. Initially by the school name. Later, just before the start, each of the rowers has their last name called as well by the loud speaker, before 'Attention, and soon after 'Go.'

-	Bow 2,	K Christopherson,	River Rowing
-	Bow 3,	S Kankel,	Los Gatos
-	Bow 4,	A Berghella,	Germantown Friends
-	Bow 5,	S Krappe,	SRC
-	Bow 6,	J Palmer,	Rye HS
-	Bow 7,	E Goffena,	Willanette RC

I follow the race closely. I video it completely again, from start to finish, with my iPhone. J Palmer in bow 6 soon gets in front by the 500 meter mark, and never relinquishes it until the finish line at the 2,000 meter mark. So Andrea once again needs to fight for 2nd place.

In fact, Andrea spends much of the time between about the 300 meters and about 1,000 in 2nd. But soon after that, S Krappe in Bow 6 comes back and surpasses Andrea. By the 1,500 mark, S Krappe is in complete command, with some light – space –

between the end of his boat, the stern, and the front point of Andrea's boat, the bow.

I keep on cheering Andrea on. But I begin to give in to the thought of him coming in 3rd, and not getting into the Semis. These top two are just too good. But Andrea is better than my hopes. He seems to find new strength. I cheer him on more to soften the blow to come in 3rd again, the top spot that does not qualify.

But wait. At the 1,750 mark is clear Andrea is closing the gap between his rival in Bow 5, Krappe, still 2nd, and him in 3rd. I begin to scream at the top of my lungs. Andrea is much faster that Bow 5. He is close, now only half a boat behind. Can he make it? I scream as hard as I can, "Andrea!!"

On the finish line, I think the boat in bow 5 got the 2nd place just by about a foot, maybe less. Andrea almost caught up completely to him. Krappe must have shit in his shorts, I think. The final official results will read:

Mens Youth 1x Rev 2:
- Bow 6,   J Palmer,   Rye HS,   7:24:535
- Bow 5,   S Krappe,   SRC,   7:31:733
- Bow 4,   A Berghella,   GFS,   7:32:380

What I'm most proud of is that Andrea gave it its best. Andrea followed my advice! He really improved a lot in those last 500 meters. He gave it all. For the first time in his rowing racing career, he came from behind. He sprinted in the last 500 meters.

It's tough to lose by such a small margin, about 6.5 tens of a second. But I consider it almost a victory seeing how Andrea came back to almost get that priced 2nd spot. Later, coach Aaron also points to the improvement in time: from over 8 minutes yesterday, to 7:32 today. Andrea had his best race, a great effort.

I go back to where the boats come back to the launch area, and wait for him. He comes back drenched. Despite not getting one of the first two spots, he has a smile on his face. He knows he did well. I yelled it to him many times. Now his coach has told him, too.

After the Rev race, he also congratulates one of the other rowers. Always the gentleman. I'm very impressed, and proud. And he does these gestures with such grace. With such poise, looking these 'colleagues' in the eyes, with firm handshakes. This attitude will serve him well. He is ready for the world.

After the race, we go out to late breakfast, basically brunch, with coach Aaron and his wonderful family. Andrea has granola and skim milk. I've had enough of yogurt, so I have Mango Waffles with whipped cream, and a Berry Delicious, a delicious smoothie.

Aaron tells us about his times at the three World Championships he rowed in. One of the most exiting one was in Milan, Italy, in one of the lakes there. He also raced in South America, for Olympic Trials, coming 7th with the top 6 going to the Olympics. He competed at the Pan American games. Clearly, he has been an elite rower, and crew is his life, which is great.

His wife, with whom he's been together forever, remembers as many details of all his competitive races around the world as he does. She said half-jokingly it is unpleasant to go out and hold hands with a rower, whose palms are always hardened up with callouses.

She and Aaron have a great family. Very tight. The 5-year old daughter is a brunette like her dad, with dark eyes, happy and cheerful. She is so exited telling us about her time at Disneyworld the day before. Bodhi, the 1-year old, is always glued to dad. A bundle of joy and affection.

I'll be forever grateful coach Aaron drove from Philadelphia to Florida with his wife and two kids. They even hauled Andrea's single boat with a trailer, the oars, all the other equipment, even his bike, which I used all the time. A huge effort, in a truck, and they even had engine problems!

After this great brunch, Andrea and I go back to the hotel and unwind. As Andrea wants to rest, I step out and walk around the splendid neighborhood, all green and flowery, and open up to my thoughts and inner self. When I come back, Andrea is still reading, but soon falls asleep. I can now write some of my first thoughts of this great trip.

Andrea's plan is to go back to see the Semifinals for the single boats. I'm proud of the fact he is not at all down he is going to see the rowers who beat him. On the contrary, he is interested to learn from them, to compare himself with the best, to test what his next goals are.

On the way back to Nathan Benderson Park, the beautiful venue in Sarasota-Bradenton where the Rowing Youth Nationals are being held, we get yogurt at Munchies. Delicious. I put a lot of strawberries and raspberries on top, to make it as healthy as I can. I'm impressed Andrea also puts strawberries on top of his, but also lots of Nutella! We do have some kind of yogurino pretty much every day in this enchanting trip.

Andrea slowly opens up during our time together. We talk, at first not much on the taxi from home to the airport. He is not a loquacious man. In fact, as any good teenager, he usually answers questions with a yes or a no, or another monosyllable. Or, even more frequently, he just shrugs his shoulders. That makes me insane. He just lifts one of his shoulders, slightly, as an answer to anything. "How was your day?" Shoulder lift. "How was the math test today?" Shoulder lift. "How was swimming?" Shoulder lift. "Is there any girl you like at school?" He pretends I never asked.

It's blistering hot at 14:44 when the first semifinal races down. We protect ourselves under the canopy by the finish line.

Mens Youth 1x Semi 1
- Bow 4,   A Morley,   Seattle RC,   7:29:581
- Bow 3,   H Formoso-Murias, Belen Jesuit 7:31:633
- Bow 5,   J Luby,   Narragansett,   7:33:774
In Bow 2, Krappe, who eliminated Andrea by less than a second, is dead last, in 7:45:282.

Mens Youth 1x Semi 2
	Bow 5,	J Puzz,	Parati,	7:27:821
-	Bow 5,	J Puzz,	Parati,	7:27:821
-	Bow 4,	S O'Brien,	Tampa,	7:28:408
-	Bow 7,	J Palmer,	Rye HS,	7:28:636

I had promised Aaron we would not stay long in the heat. After the races, we quickly get back in the car. We drive to the movies. We see Love and Mercy, an interesting movie about the story of Brian Wilson, the lead of the band Beach Boys. An interesting story about the thin line between genius and madness, as he has a schizoaffective disorder.

We are late for dinner, which is set for 6pm at a great place in Sarasota, called Crab and Fin. My colleague the surgeon John Kairys had invited us to join his family hours before. As we arrive, they offer us some of their appetizers, including alligator, which is a bit chewy.

The other three at the table for 6 are John's wife, their daughter Lauren and a friend of hers, a fellow rower. Andrea likes John's daughter, one can sense it right away. She is very much an extrovert, has transparent blue eyes, a ready smile, auburn reddish hair, a captivating personality.

I put my foot in my mouth with her about Harvard, saying many kids there are depressed, got there only because pushed by their parents, and statistics show they have very few romantic or sexual relationships while in college. As she is going to Temple, in Philadelphia, from two physician parents, I think I'm offering support. Then John gets back in the conversation, saying he went to Harvard for college. Oh… I'm so dumb. I feel like a fool. John is super-nice about it.

After dinner I notice is still day outside, the sun still up in the sky, warm. I see a sign that say something related to the beach. I decide to drive to it, and Andrea almost surprisingly does not offer too much resistance. We find parking luckily right by the shore. We talk sitting down by the beautiful sunset.

Once again, Andrea opens up. He is serene. We have a great discussion on the beach about falling in love. He falls in love like I do, losing himself completely. Beautiful. I tell him I highly admire him for that. I recount my failed attempts to get my feelings exchanged back from Paola, the green-eyed girl sitting in the front row in middle school. Or from Caterina, the blue-eyed, black-hair sunshine of a girl who I was crazy about at the end of middle school, and who instead became a noun after high school.

Or Annalisa, the blue-eyed 14-year old from Bologna who I met in Cambridge, U.K., when I was 16 and in high school, with whom I only got to hold hands for a day before she told me she was not ready for a relationship. Love is great, but love does hurt too. I tell him to continue to fall in love, as it is one of the best, if not the best, feeling one can ever experience.

Paola – my wife – calls. We manage to do a FaceTime. She is having dinner at a friends' house. We talk with Arturo, the common friend who first introduced us in 1993. They are all at dinner at Luigi Grasso's house. These are definitively some of my best friends, guys I highly admire.

Then Luigi Bagella asks Andrea and I if the water is warm. The temptation is too great. Once my foot detects the water is super warm, even more than it would be in my beloved Adriatic in the evening, I quickly decide to take my clothes off, and jump in the water. This is the true me. A true lover of life. Nobody is surprised. I feel refreshed, alive, anew.

Once back at the hotel, Andrea as usual wants to get to sleep early. I shower, we read a bit, and well before 10pm the lights in out meager hotel room at the Ramada Inn are off.

It's the third and last day of racing, Sunday, June 14, 2015. I'm a bit sad, as this time one-on-one with Andrea has been fantastic. There is nothing like spending time with someone you love. Just the two of you. It's proven that to get something done, to invent something, to manage a project, a team of 4-8 is best. But I think that souls open up best when the discourse is just with only one other brain. You can look each other in the face. You only have to trust one other human. You expect no surprises, as the feedback is coming straight from where you are looking at.

Look even at the current mania with texting. It's best among two people. Even if you do not have the other across physically from you, you can reach high levels of communication, of exchange, of soul-cleansing, when you bare yourself to someone you love, you trust, you are truly friends with. One-on-one.

It's another splendid morning in Florida. The temperature feels just a degree or so cooler than the day before. There is only the most minimal of morning breezes. The first day Friday the water of this man-made basin here was completely flat.

Andrea had a bit of diarrhea that first day. He has been pooping regularly, today at least twice this morning. I feel like the manager of a star athlete. I have to manage his rest, his food intake, his safety, his bowel habits, his hydration status, his mindfulness.

His race today is at 8:22am. It's the C Final. I feel like the racetrack now is our new home. We begin to recognize faces, people. The Indiana rower, 6'6" or so, perhaps the only junior better than Andrea, passes us by with his coach. On the other side, we eye the Belen guy, from Miami, who beat Andrea at the Scholastic Nationals on the Cooper River in New Jersey, and has qualified for the A Final, with a great chance to medal. So, to recap, the A Final has the best 6 rowers so far. The B Final has rowers 7th to 12th.

I'm so proud of Andrea. He made it here to the nationals. He had a couple of great races already, especially the second one. Out of 22 top rowers in the US, he is among the top 18. Now, being in the C Final, he has a chance to get to be the 13th best high school single rower in the US. Not bad for a junior, who started rowing just about 16 months ago, and has really only trained as a rower for a total of less than 8 months, the spring of 2014 and this one of 2015.

The Mens Youth 1x C Final line up:
- Bow 2,   L Kankel,   Los Gatos
- Bow 3,   E Sammons,   Saratoga
- Bow 4,   A Berghella,   Germantown Friends
- Bow 5,   P McKendall,   Narragansett
- Bow 6,   E Goffena,   Williamette RC
- Bow 7,   L Sendelbach, Orange County

It's less than an hour before the Final. Andrea stands up and begins to do the warming exercises. Mostly light stretching. His coach follows his every move. Leaves him alone at times, but often goes over and talks to him, just to ease his mind in the race. All around Andrea, slick long boats, tall thin athletes.

As he brings with Aaron his boat to the launch, the officials check him and the boat out. It seems like every day the security check is more detailed. They check his wristband for name and school. His garments. His boat up and down. They even look inside the boat, despite having to go under it as the boat is upside down on Aaron's and Andrea's shoulders.

High stakes. The Finals of the High School Nationals. I'm thrilled just to be here and watch the show. Everyone is so serious. Everyone has his or her game face on. Most rowers have their earphones on, and are trying to relax with whatever music. Not many smiles. It's pre-race. It's game time.

From a table afar, I watch Andrea doing the last stretches. He prepares his boat, now on the water. He places his butt pad on the seat. He puts the oars in. Carefully, swiftly, he positions himself in the boat. Aaron is couched near him with the last pieces of advice. Yesterday he got 3rd instead of 2nd because he did not increase his stroke rate in the last 50 meters. Aaron wants to make sure Andrea has his oars in the water at the finish line. A bit like Michael Phelps did with his last stroke when he won one of Olympic golds by one one hundredth of a second.

As I see Andrea row off the launch, I get to the bike, and ride to the starting line. It's a great time, full of excitement, about 3 miles with adrenaline pumping stronger and stronger inside of me. I know Andrea wants to win today. Indeed he can win. He is coming with the best time of the 6 rowers in the C Final. I want him to feel proud of himself at the end. This is the last race of the season. It would be great to finish on a high.

Today there are more and more people out. Even biking. You can feel a bit of tension in the air. The temperature is slowly rising already, it's warm, humid. It's Florida in mid-June. But it's a gorgeous day for sports. I hope it's an unforgettable day for Andrea.

I admire the venue. It's really majestic. Designed just for rowing. Elegant. Long. Comfortable for rowers, spectators, officials. I arrive at the starting line when the Women 1x A Final has already started. Following it, it's Andrea's race.

The six rowers line up perfectly. Andrea, as usual, seems to be the most nervous one. Once in position, he continues to look around him, especially behind him, to study the line of water where he'll have to stay in. Then he looks back in front of him at his boat. Then he turns again. And again. And again.

Most of the other rowers seem to just be leaning forward with their upper torso, staring at their lap, seemingly praying. Young officials are holding their boats in perfect positions, as many other officials around them, in boats, on land, on an overlooking tower, with cameras everywhere, study their every move.

Mens Youth 1x C Final

Bow 2,	S Kankel,	Los Gatos
Bow 3,	E Sammons,	Saratoga
Bow 4,	A Berghella,	Germantown Friends
Bow 5,	P McKendall,	Narragansett
Bow 6,	E Goffena,	Willamette RC
Bow 7,	L Sendelbach,	Orange County

The loud speaker greets every rower by his name. Then begins to update them about how long to the start. "Seven minutes." Then an interminable silence in the air. All is still. "Six minutes," the speakers almost wake us all from meditation. "Five minutes," wow, still so long to wait... "Four minutes," I think they are just building nervousness in the athletes. "Three minutes," making progress. "Two minutes," we are almost there. "One minute," oh... here we go.

The loud speaker starts saying their names again, one by one. When she says, "Mister Berghella" my heart sinks. This is it Andrea. Man you are famous and important. "Attention," then a short pause, oh Andrea please do well, for yourself, give it your best... "Go!"

Andrea has a decent start. The first day, Friday, he said he had swerved off, had not gone straight at the start, and had to readjust. I think today the start looks better. He is certainly not first off, but he never is. But by the first 100 meters he is among the 3 or 4 up front. They are lined up parallel to each other.

The race seems to be very tight. Andrea is near or at the front at the 250 meters, but there are at least three other rowers right up there with him. In other races, by this time, the leader had established himself, and usually never given up the lead. Our coach Aaron says that it is easier to 'row from the front,' as in the lead you can control what the others are doing, pace yourself to give just enough to be up front, and see any attach early, so to be better able to counterattack and stay first.

Andrea has the best qualifying time coming in this C Final. He is in line 4, which is where the official put the boat that they think will win. But Andrea is not decisively in front even at the 500 meters. He is up there, but surrounded by the other boats. I begin to wonder if he'll once again come in 3rd, or maybe 2nd, but not win today, either.

There are at least three bikers, among others, next to me, who are screaming "Spencer!! Go Spencer!!" I'm not sure which one is Spencer. But I make sure I pass them on my bike, and watch the race from the front. I do not want to trail them. I want to be lined up while I bike with the rower in first, which is not Andrea, but at least I'll have a better view at the finish line of who comes in first.

At the 750 meters Andrea is leading by a quarter or a half a boat-length. There are at least four other boats around him, less than a boat length behind. It's a very tight race. I also know Andrea often has is best position in the first 1,000 meters, and so I fear things can only get worse, this is the best he can do.

I scream loudly my first, "Go Andrea!!" The other bikers behind me have been screaming "Spencer" for a while. I feel Andrea deserves some cheering on already, even if I usually stay mostly quiet in the first half of a race. Andrea is ever slightly up front.

At the 1,000 meters mark, the boats are all six still within a couple of boat lengths. It's a very tight race. I scream again, "Bravo Andrea!! Bravissimo!!" He is still first. But the boat in line 2 seems to be attaching strongly now. Bow (line) 2, closest to me, is now parallel to Andrea at about 1,100 meter mark. Later I'll find out this is indeed where Spencer is, from Los Gatos, a famous rowing club from the Bay Area. They are one of the best teams in the nation, as we heard when we recently visited San Francisco. Spencer's boat is a beautiful aqua green.

In Bow 5, further away from Andrea's boat from my vantage point, Mister Goffena is also making a move, less powerful than Bow 2, but enough to also be parallel to Andrea. Now three boats seem to be sharing the lead. Oh man, this is so tight, not what I was hoping.

I see Andrea is struggling a bit. I scream, "Quick through the middle Andre'!" Coach Aaron had said that after the first 1,000 meters Andrea seems to get tired. And so when he pulls the oars towards his chest he does not do so as quickly as he should, especially in the first half of his pulling, pulling hardest and quick only at the end.

"Dai Andrea!," in Italian, I also yell, as he is still tied for first with Bow 2 and Bow 5. They are floating well on the water, and it's impossible to say yet who has more in the tank. "Keep you back straight!" Aaron had said to remind him of this.

I had wanted not to scream too much, but the race is super tight. I feel that if I pretend that Andrea gives it his very best effort, I also have to give it my best. From now until the finish line, I scream cheers continuously, only in Italian now, so the others rowers cannot understand. In fact, at some point, I hear Spencer's family members say, "What the hell is he saying?" and of course I smile a bit inside, feeling advantaged.

After the 1,000 meters, Spencer in Bow 2 continues to even more decisively take off. By the 1,250 meter mark, he is in a solid first by a full boat length over Andrea. "Spacca Andrea!! Dai!!" I keep on cheering Andrea on, but it does not seem to work. I do not care. I just want Andrea to be proud of himself at the end. 14th, 15th, or whatever, I just want him to give his best.

Spencer now has put some light between his stern and Andrea's bow. Spencer's family is cheering, but only a bit, since the race seems in Spencer's control. So I take over the screaming, at least proud to win the cheering fight, even if it's one of me and many of them.

At the 1,500 meter mark, Spencer in Bow 2 has a boat and a half lead over Andrea. I scream louder my cheering for Andrea. I let him know it's the last 500 meters, to give it now his best. Historically this is where he loses races, when he does not do well. But yesterday he had a great last 500 meters. I just have little to no hope he can catch first place Spencer, who is so far ahead, with so little to go.

Up to the 1,700 meters, Spencer in his slick light aqua boat near me is still in front with light between his boat and Andrea in 2nd. Andrea is holding though. He had been losing ground to Bow 2 since the 1,000 meter mark. Now not anymore. "Bravo Andrea!!" "Leave everything you have on the water!!" My screaming, all in Italian, is continuous until the end.

The boats are now in front of all the stands and crowd of these Youth National High School Rowing Championships. The noise level increases. One can even hear the excited official announcer calling the race from the loud speaker. It feels like we are in a choreographed thrilling last scene of a movie, full of emotions and suspense.

At 1,800 meters, Andrea's bow seems to be touching the line of Spencer's stern. Still behind by a perfect boat length, but not losing anymore, maybe gaining a few inches. Meanwhile, Bow 5 has made a strong move, and is just a tiny less than a boat length behind Andrea. I begin to fear Andrea may not even come in 2nd.

I'm screaming at the top of my lungs. Many Italian curse words come out of my mouth. I'm sure I'm read in the face, still on my bike, no hands on the steering wheel, videoing every second of this great race. "Vai porca puttana, dai cazzo, dai Andre', sei forte, vai!!!" I feel my throat hurts, and I'm actually losing my voice.

It's probably the same sensation Andrea is feeling. His muscles must be aching. He must feel he is at the end of his rope. He must be digging deep. If he can find this inner strength in adversity, this power after seemingly all was already spent, I can for sure keep on screaming at the top of my lungs, even injuring my vocal cords, who cares. Now or never.

Now Andrea is flying on the water, at the 1,850 and 1,900 meters, he does find new speed. I can tell he is pulling on those oars with ever more vigor. His stroke rate is steadily increasing, meaning is his doing more strokes per minutes, moving his oars more quickly. Now his boat is beginning to overlap Spencer's!!!

By the 1,900 meters, he is only half a boat behind the lead, Spencer, in Bow 2.

It's hard to believe my eyes. I could not dream of a better, more thrilling scenario. I'm screaming "Andrea!! Dai ora!! Forza cazzo!! Sei il migliore!! Lascia tutto qui!!!" Spencer's family slowly seems to have lost their serenity. They go quiet. I'm screaming much more than all of them combined. I feel like I'm the only one the rowers can hear. I also hear Aaron, the coach, all the way on the other side of the racing course, yells his obscenities, him in English. The name "Andrea" resonates in the air from all over.

"Forte, dai!! Cosi'!! Bravo!! Bravo, bravissimo!!" I am screaming continuously, without taking a breath. Andrea is definitively gaining. "Vola Andrea, dai, vola!!" (Fly Andrea, come on, fly!!) Now he is less than half a boat length from Spencer, still in the lead in Bow 2. "Vai Andrea, dai, bravo!!"

They are in the last 50 meters. It's hard to believe my eyes, who are watching the race from the iPhone I'm still holding in my hands while I bike. Andrea's bow is now in line with Spencer's. And Andrea is gaining, definitively going faster. He has found another gear. He is flying on the water. The guy from San Francisco does not hold his position. Soon Andrea's bow is in front, first by just an inch, then two, then a foot!!!

I can see now the orange buoys of the finish line in my iPhone screen. Andrea is in first. I cannot believe my eyes. The boat in lane 5 is also going very fast, gaining for sure, mostly on lane 2, and is just half a boat away from Andrea's. Andrea's bow is the first to cross the line of orange buoys, in the middle of the other two boats. I'm sure of it: HE WON!!!!

"Cazzo, bravo, bravo!!! Bravissimo" I basically fall off the bike, the video I checked later is at this time all blurred and messed up. I'm still screaming, "Bravissimo Andrea!!! Campione, campione!!!" Tears well in my eyes. "Campione del mondo!! Bravo, bravo!!" Emotions overwhelm me. "Bravo Madonna, sei il piu' grande!!"

I'm so proud of him. Especially because he came from behind. Because he followed our advice. Because he gave it his best. He increased his effort. He revved up his stroke rate. He left everything he had on the water. He showed the world, or at least the United States, what he can do.

Mens Youth 1x C Final
1. Bow 4, A Berghella,   Germantown Friends, 7:39:904
2. Bow 5, P McKendall,   Narragansett,   7:40:603
3. Bow 2, S Kankel,   Los Gatos,   7:41:434
4. Bow, 7, L Sendelbach,   Orange County,   7:46:662
5. Bow 6, E Goffena,   Willamette RC,   7:46:662
6. Bow 3, E Sammons,   Saratoga,   7:49:770

I'm so excited. I am still crying from joy. I cannot control the tears. My emotions. I'm so happy for Andrea. He fully deserved it. Later, the Columbia College coach will email him, impressed he was able to come from behind and finish such a thrilling sprint, in such a close national race.

I follow Andrea from the bike, as he rows back to the finishing boat launch. Now away from the stand, I do not have to yell anymore. With a broken voice, hoarse from screaming, and still wet from the tears, I congratulate him again. I can see he is smiling despite the endeavor. There is nothing better than a feeling of accomplishment after such a great effort.

It has been an amazing weekend. Andrea got better every race. He shaved off almost 30 seconds from the first to the second race, and almost caught up to the 2nd place finisher in the second (Rep) race, with a much better last 500 meters. But this last and third race has been the masterpiece.

In this Final, he really gave it all. He learned from his races at Cooper in New Jersey, when he lost his 2nd place finish in the last 10 meters, to finish 4th. He learned from these first two Youth national races, as he began to do a bit better in the last 500 meters, but not enough to overcome those in front of him.

This is what life is all about. Andrea worked very hard at something he enjoys, and likes to do well in. Thanks to good coaching, and many hours on the boat, and on the erg machine on land, he mastered sculling on a single boat, at least for a junior high schooler. And he was lucky and good to find a perfect event, on a national venue, to show his skills. He deserves all our admiration, and pat on the back. Bravo!